D0423097

GIRLFRIENDS

GIRLFRIENDS

a celebration

Lawrence Teacher Books
Philadelphia

Copyright ©2005 by Lawrence Teacher Books

Printed in China. All rights reserved.

Mechanicals produced by book soup publishing, inc.

Cover and interior design by Carole Goodman/BLUE ANCHOR DESIGN

Quotes compiled by Melissa Lieberman
Edited by Erin Slonaker

This book may not be reproduced in any form or by any means without written permission of the publisher.

ISBN 1-930408-03-X

10 9 8 7 6 5 4 3 2 1

Please support your local book or gift store. However, if you cannot find this book there, you may order it directly from the publisher. Please add $1.50 for postage and handling. Send check or money order to the address below.

LAWRENCE TEACHER BOOKS
1 PEARL BUCK COURT, BRISTOL, PA 19007

introduction

There's a magical bond that unites women in friendship. We may have different goals, different lives, and different opinions, but somewhere deep down we find that the similarities we share are the most important.

It's with our girlfriends that we find solace from the rest of the world. We go to each other for comfort, for support, and even for a laugh. Many of us plan a special "girls' night out" whenever possible.

When we're with our girl-friends, more than any other relationship, we find that it's easiest to be just who we are and nothing more.

Together we can discuss anything and everything, from politics to fashion to philosophy to relationships. Our perspective as women lends a unique insight on any topic we choose. We are always learning from our girlfriends, becoming better people, better women.

This little book is a collection of quotes from women honoring that special bond, those special friends whom we call *girlfriends.*

True friendship between women is rare, I know, but we were never disloyal.

Anita Brookner
BRITISH WRITER
(B. 1928)

I found real love in girlfriends.

Tina Turner

AMERICAN SINGER

(B. 1938)

I always felt that the great high privilege, relief, and comfort of friendship was that one had to explain nothing.

Katherine Mansfield
BRITISH WRITER
(1888–1923)

We were united by a common bond of interest. We spoke each other's language.

Ruth Rowland Nichols
AMERICAN AVIATOR
(1901–1961)

Female friendships are like no other relationship: unconditional, loving, silly, silly, safe. They are our secret weapon.

Beverly Lowry

20TH CENTURY AMERICAN WRITER

The connections between and among women are the most feared, the most problematic, and the most potentially transforming force on the planet.

Adrienne Rich
AMERICAN POET
(B. 1929)

In the world of relationships, possibly the most complicated, uncommon, hard to find, hard to keep, and most rewarding has got to be friendship.

Lauren Bacall
AMERICAN ACTOR
(B. 1924)

Friendship is about commitment and loyalty. I don't think it matters how far apart you are. I don't see some of my girlfriends for ages, but when we get together it is as if time hasn't passed.

Frances Barber

BRITISH ACTRESS

(B. 1958)

The growth of true friendship may be a lifelong affair.

Sarah Orne Jewett
AMERICAN WRITER
(1849–1909)

Now I seem to have a pack of real-life female buddies, these smart, intelligent women who are celebrating the power of female friendship—girlfriend power.

Rebecca Wells

20TH CENTURY AMERICAN WRITER

We need old friends to help us grow old and new friends to help us stay young.

Letty Cottin Pogrebin
AMERICAN WRITER
(B. 1939)

The most called-upon prerequisite of a friend is an accessible ear.

Maya Angelou
AMERICAN WRITER
(B. 1928)

If one could be friendly with women, what a pleasure—the relationship so secret and private compared with relations with men.

Virginia Woolf
BRITISH WRITER
(1882–1941)

After an acquaintance of ten minutes many women will exchange confidences that a man would not reveal to a lifelong friend.

Page Smith

AMERICAN HISTORIAN, WRITER

(B. 1917)

Girls and women become more authentic through their friends.

Pat Ross

AMERICAN WRITER

(B. 1943)

SISTERS

It's been wonderful to have a best friend who knew me before this whirlwind. Somebody I can go home to. Somebody who knows what's real.

Jennifer Aniston
AMERICAN ACTOR
(B. 1969)

. . . as nobody can do more mischief to a woman than a woman, so perhaps might one reverse the maxim and say nobody can do more good.

Lady Elizabeth Holland
BRITISH SALONIST
(1771–1845)

The bond between women is a circle—we are together within it.

Judy Grahn

AMERICAN POET, WRITER

(B. 1940)

What would we do without our women friends? I can't imagine how we could survive without the hugs and humor, the closeness and Kleenex that our female friendships provide.

Cokie Roberts

AMERICAN NEWS ANALYST

(B. 1943)

My friends have made the story of my life.

Helen Keller

AMERICAN WRITER, EDUCATOR

(1880–1968)

The depth of a friendship—how much it means to us—depends, at least in part, upon how many parts of ourselves a friend sees, shares, and validates.

Lillian Rubin

20TH CENTURY AMERICAN WRITER

Lots of people want to ride with you in the limo, but what you want is someone who will take the bus with you when the limo breaks down.

Oprah Winfrey
AMERICAN ACTOR,
TALK-SHOW HOST
(B. 1954)

Good books, like good friends, are few and chosen; the more select, the more enjoyable.

Louisa May Alcott
AMERICAN WRITER
(1832–1888)

We have a great respect for each other and we trust each other. That's what a great friendship is, whether we talk every day or not.

Jennifer Azzi
AMERICAN PRO BASKETBALL PLAYER
(B. 1969)

True friendship is like phosphorescence—it glows best when the world around you goes dark.

Denise Martin
AMERICAN WRITER
(B. 1940)

We rarely talk of sex the way men do, in terms of I've had this one, I've had that one. There's a friend I've known for 19 years and all I've known of her private life is what I've heard from others.

Jeanne Moreau
FRENCH ACTRESS
(B. 1928)

Understand that friendship arrives from the least likely sources and flourishes in the least likely locations. Understand that someone can know you very well though you have not told her about yourself.

Whitney Otto
AMERICAN WRITER
(B. 1955)

We know that we are all bound by the life stories we divulge to our friends, whether they be about the highs, the lows, or even the in-betweens of life. We nod with sympathetic murmurs and accept the truth because we truly love each other, we women do.

Lois Wyse

AMERICAN WRITER,
ADVERTISING EXECUTIVE
(B. 1926)

Each friend represents a world in us, a world possibly not born until they arrive, and it is only by this meeting that a new world is born.

Anaïs Nin

FRENCH-AMERICAN WRITER

(1903-1977)

It is curious that it may be the help of a housekeeper and a friend that facilitates a woman's life work, while the closest analogy . . . one would find from the pen of a man is typically a tribute to his wife.

Alice Rossi

AMERICAN EDUCATOR, WRITER

(B. 1922)

It is a rare and special thing to find a friend who will remain a friend forever.

Ruth Langdon Morgan
AMERICAN WRITER
(1878–1940)

As time went on, we grew stronger together and became like sisters. It was nice having somebody around that I could trust and tell anything to, knowing it would stay with her until she leaves this planet.

Patti LaBelle
AMERICAN SINGER
(B. 1944)

It seemed to me that those women were conducting the most important business in the world as they talked together and that they were having a whole lot of fun doing it. The warm, reciprocal, nurturing friendship they shared was one of the reasons I wanted to grow up to be a woman.

Susan Koppelman
20TH CENTURY AMERICAN WRITER, EDITOR, EDUCATOR

Often intimacies between women go backwards, beginning with revelations and ending up in small-talk without loss of esteem.

Elizabeth Bowen
BRITISH WRITER
(1899–1973)

Girls' emotional lives are lived with their girlfriends.

Terri Apter
20TH CENTURY BRITISH WRITER, PSYCHOLOGIST,

& Ruthellen Josselson
20TH CENTURY AMERICAN WRITER, PSYCHOTHERAPIST

It's mutual support once the competition is ruled out. With women friendships, you're comrades in the battle of life.
Miriam Lacob
20TH CENTURY SOUTH AFRICAN WRITER

Her deepest heart's desire cannot be satisfied by the circum-stances of her birth, by material finery, by a father, a mother, or a brother, but only by a friendship of her choosing with another girl.

Amy Ling

20TH CENTURY AMERICAN WRITER, PROFESSOR

Friendships aren't perfect and yet they are precious.

Letty Cottin Pogrebin
AMERICAN WRITER
(B. 1939)

After the age of forty there isn't much to live for except friendship.

Francine du Plessix Gray

POLISH-AMERICAN WRITER

(B. 1930)

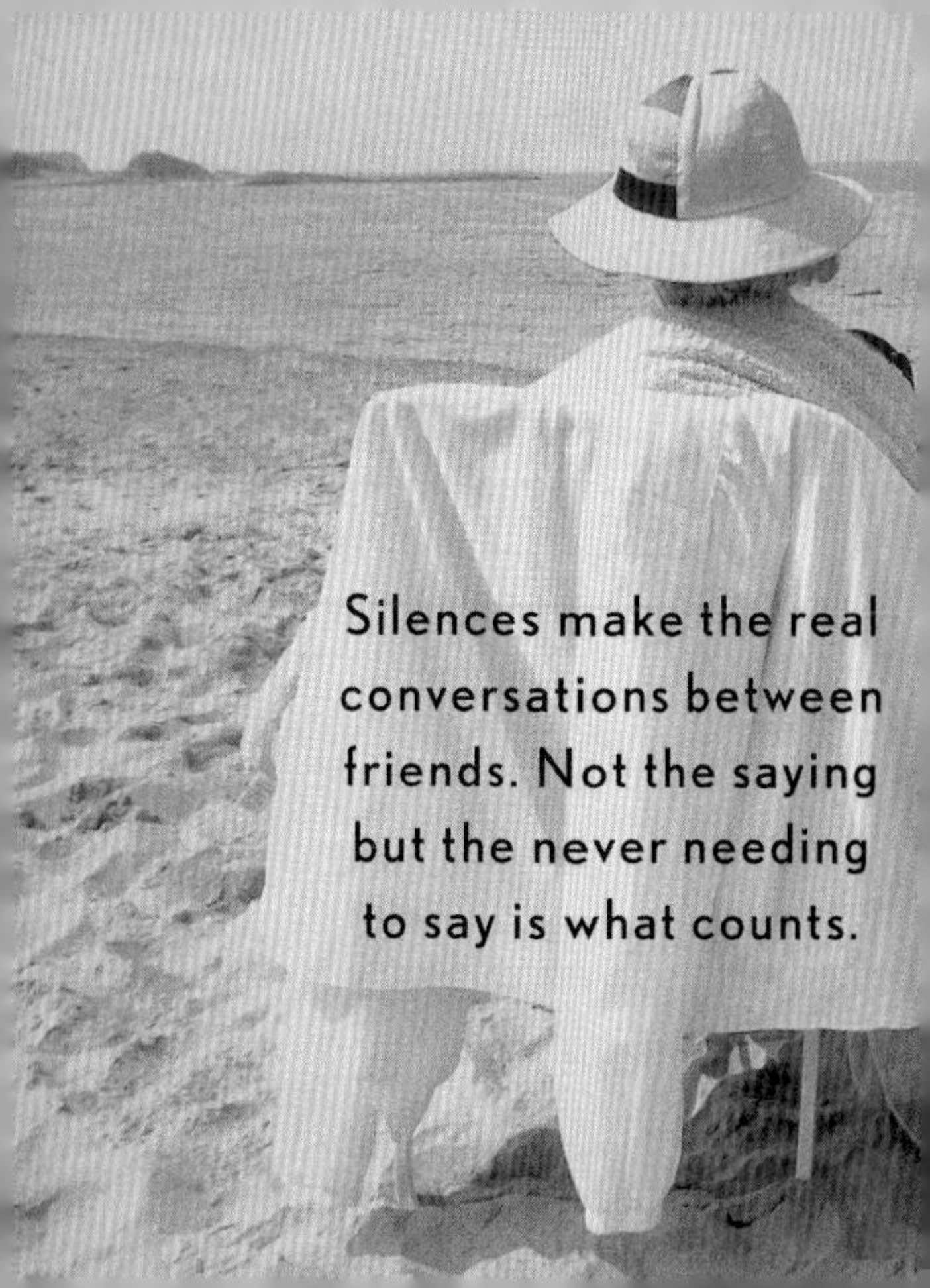
Silences make the real
conversations between
friends. Not the saying
but the never needing
to say is what counts.

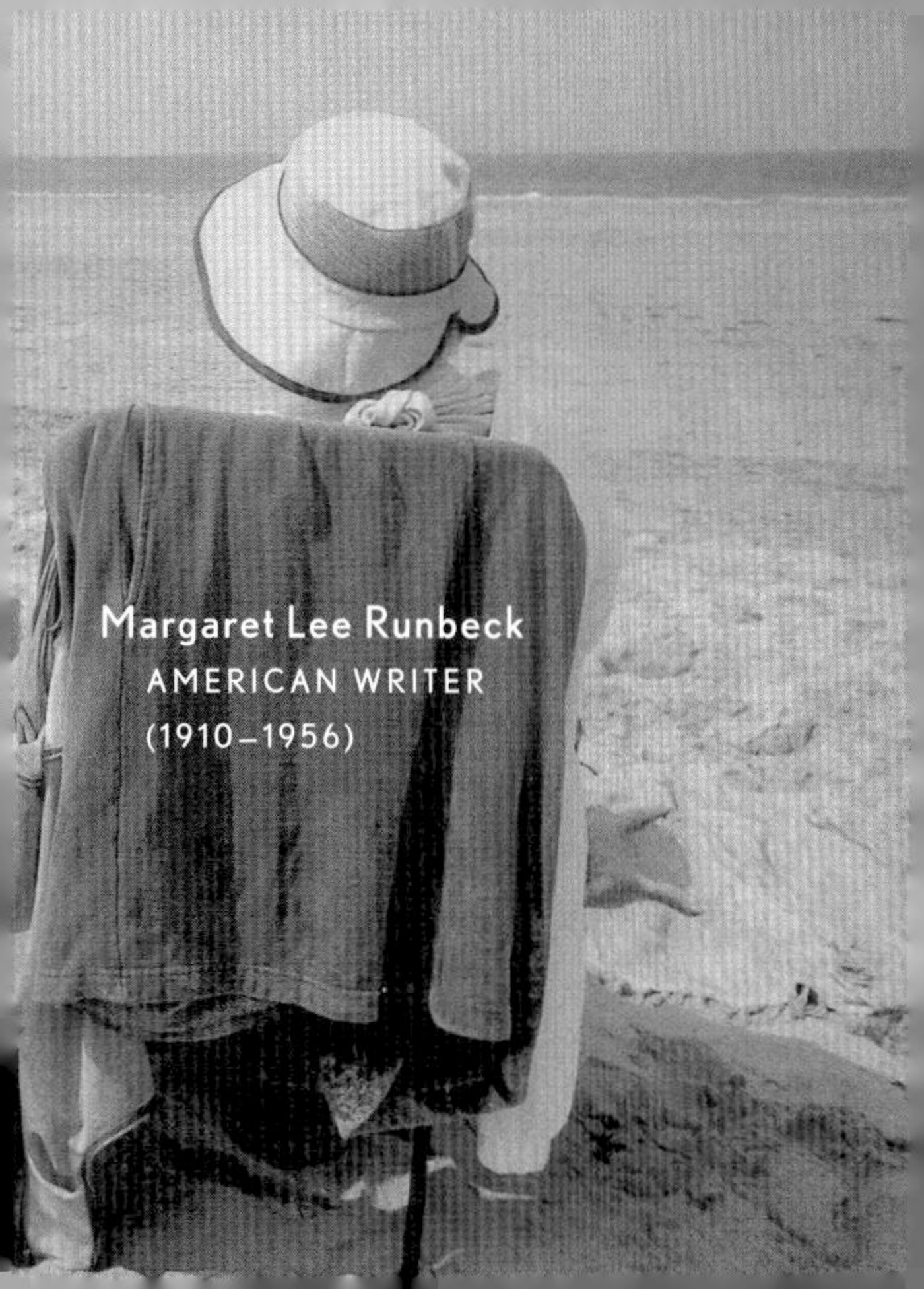

Margaret Lee Runbeck

AMERICAN WRITER

(1910–1956)

True friends are those who really know you but love you anyway.

Edna Buchanan

AMERICAN JOURNALIST

(B. 1946)

The loneliest woman in the world is a woman without a close woman friend.

Toni Morrison
AMERICAN WRITER
(B. 1931)

Friendship's a noble name, 'tis love refined.

Susannah Centlivre

BRITISH PLAYWRIGHT

(1669–1723)

Even in old age, these two women nurtured their friendship. They kept a steady stream of notes and gifts flowing between them, relishing the comfort and joy of a lifelong friendship.

Margaret Truman
AMERICAN FIRST DAUGHTER
(B. 1924)

You can date the evolving life of a mind, like the age of a tree, by the rings of friendship formed by the expanding central trunk.

Mary McCarthy
AMERICAN WRITER
(1912–1989)

Great friendships with women are some of life's most difficult and caring intimacies. If I work harder at them, I hope to have them forever.

Wendy Wasserstein
AMERICAN PLAYWRIGHT
(B. 1950)

You don't know a woman until you have had a letter from her.

Ada Leverson

BRITISH WRITER

(1862–1933)

When the sun shines on you, you see your friends. Friends are the thermometers by which one may judge the temperature of our fortunes.

Lady Marguerite Blessington
IRISH WRITER
(1789–1849)

Female friendships that work are relationships in which women help each other belong to themselves.

Louise Bernikow
AMERICAN WRITER
(B. 1940)

I don't think any woman in power really has a happy life unless she's got a large number of women friends—because you sometimes must go and sit down and let down your hair with someone you can trust totally.

Margaret Thatcher
BRITISH PRIME MINISTER
(B. 1925)

Few comforts are more alluring for a woman than the rich intimate territory of women's talk. A woman friend will say, "You are not alone. I have felt that way, too. This is what happened to me." Home, in other words.

Elsa Walsh

AMERICAN JOURNALIST, WRITER

(B. 1959)

There were equal measures of comfort and amusement in our communications; I think it is safe to say that we delighted in one another.

Jane Hamilton

AMERICAN WRITER

(B. 1957)

Is there a dearer
name than friend?
Think of it for me.

Abigail Adams

AMERICAN FIRST LADY

(1744–1818)

When I was younger, I had more male friends than female friends. Now I've come to realize how rewarding women friends can be. There can be real love between girlfriends.

Donna Mills

AMERICAN ACTOR

(B. 1943)

Only by becoming friends with other women, by understanding what we share and don't share, can we truly begin to know what it is to be a woman today.

Judith Finlayson
20TH CENTURY AMERICAN WRITER

Girls especially are fond of exchanging confidences with those who they think they can trust; it is one of the most charming traits of a simple, earnesthearted girlhood, and they are the happiest women who never lose it entirely.

Lucy Larcom
AMERICAN POET, MILL WORKER
(1824–1893)

My girlfriends are the sisters I picked out for myself.

Mary-Margaret Martinez
AMERICAN WRITER
(B. 1960)

Friends, no matter how far separated, will grow in love and sympathy and nearness to each other.

Bertha Conde

EARLY 20TH CENTURY AMERICAN WRITER

I am treating you as my friend, asking you to share my present minuses in the hope I can ask you to share my future pluses.

Katherine Mansfield
BRITISH WRITER
(1888-1923)

Femininity means different things to different women, but being able to celebrate your own womanhood helps you celebrate your women friends.

Carmen Renee Berry
& Tamara Traeder
20TH CENTURY AMERICAN WRITERS

The pieces I am,
she gather them
and give them
back to me in all
the right order.

from *Beloved* by
Toni Morrison
AMERICAN WRITER
(B. 1931)

We've been friends longer than we've been people; she's the sister I never had.

Suzanne Finnamore

20TH CENTURY AMERICAN WRITER

We shelter our children for a time; we live side by side with men; and that is all. We owe them nothing, and are owed nothing. I think we owe our friends more, especially our female friends.

Fay Weldon
BRITISH WRITER
(B. 1933)

The friends one's mother chooses for herself lets her daughter see what grown-up female life is like.

Christine O'Hagan

20TH CENTURY AMERICAN WRITER

Through becoming her friend I became a better person, and she said the same of me.

Amanda Cross

AMERICAN WRITER

(B. 1926)

I think women know how to be friends. That's what saves our lives.

Alice Adams
AMERICAN WRITER
(B. 1926)

Friendship between women can take different forms. It can run like a river, quietly and sustainingly through life; it can be an intermittent, sometime thing; or it can explode like a meteor, altering the atmosphere so that nothing ever feels or looks the same again.

Molly Haskell

AMERICAN CRITIC

(B. 1939)

And we find at the end of a perfect day, the soul of a friend we've made.

Carrie Jacobs Bond
AMERICAN COMPOSER
(1862–1946)

She became for me an island of light, fun wisdom where I could run with my discoveries and torments and hopes at any time of day and find welcome.

May Sarton

AMERICAN POET, WRITER

(1912–1995)

One is taught by experience to put a premium on those few people who can appreciate you for what you are.

Gail Godwin

AMERICAN WRITER

(B. 1937)

Our female friends are forever.

Anna Quindlen

AMERICAN WRITER, COLUMNIST

(B. 1953)

She always knows exactly what I need to boost my spirits and is forever doing the things that bring huge smiles to my face.

Aimee Olivo
AMERICAN WRITER
(B. 1941)

Men kick friendship around like a football, but it doesn't seem to crack. Women treat it like glass and it goes to pieces.

Anne Morrow Lindbergh
AMERICAN WRITER
(B. 1906)

But every road
is tough for me /
That has no friend
to cheer it.

Elizabeth Shane

EARLY 20TH CENTURY IRISH POET

Everyone has a gift for something, even if it is the gift of being a good friend.

Marian Anderson
AMERICAN SINGER
(1902–1993)

The friend who holds your hand and says the wrong thing is made of dearer stuff than the one who stays away.

Barbara Kingsolver
AMERICAN WRITER
(B. 1955)

The most beautiful discovery true friends make is that they can grow separately without growing apart.

Elisabeth Foley
20TH CENTURY AMERICAN WRITER

Many women understand. We may share experiences, make jokes, paint pictures, and describe humiliations that mean little to men, but women understand.

Gloria Steinem

AMERICAN ACTIVIST, EDITOR, WRITER

(B. 1934)

She made me believe in myself. She was hysterically loud and loved noise and a good time. She made me feel okay to be who I was.

Bette Midler

AMERICAN ACTRESS, SINGER

(B. 1945)

Most women would agree. Our friends are among life's greatest treasures. They help us negotiate the difficult hurdles of life.

Brenda Hunter

20TH CENTURY AMERICAN WRITER

In meeting again after a separation, acquaintances ask after our outward life, friends after our inner life.

Marie von Ebner-Eschenbach
AUSTRIAN WRITER
(1830–1916)

Women's friendships often have the intensity of romantic attachment.

Lucy O'Brien
20TH CENTURY BRITISH WRITER

I suppose there is one friend in the life of each of us who seems not a separate person, however dear and beloved, but an expansion, an interpretation, of one's self, the very meaning of one's soul.

Edith Wharton
AMERICAN WRITER
(1862–1937)

Photo Credits

Page 10: ©Telegraph Colour Library (FPG International)
Page 17: ©Telegraph Colour Library (FPG International)
Page 20: ©Telegraph Colour Library (FPG International)
Pages 28–29: ©Sharon Wohlmuth
Pages 34–35: ©Sharon Wohlmuth
Page 40: ©VGC (FPG International)
Pages 48–49: ©Elma Garcia (Photonica)
Pages 56–57: ©Ellen Denuto (Photonica)
Page 62: ©The Picture Book (Photonica)
Page 68: ©Beverly Brown (Photonica)
Page 74: ©1997 Keyvan Behpour (Photonica)
Pages 78–79: ©Masayuki Nakajima (Photonica)
Pages 84–85: ©Karen Cipolla (Photonica)
Page 91: ©1993 Dennie Cody (FPG International)
Pages 98–99: ©Daniel Proctor (Photonica)
Page 106: ©1998 Laura Dick (FPG International)
Page 112: ©Telegraph Colour Library (FPG International)
Pages 116–117: ©1997 Ron Chapple (FPG International)